P9-BYE-604

Captain James Cook

by Ruth Harley
illustrated by Monroe Eisenberg

Troll Associates

CARLOCK SCHOOL IMC

Copyright© 1979 by Troll Associates
All rights reserved. No part of this book may be used or reproduced
in any manner whatsoever without written permission from the publisher.
Printed in the United States of America.

Troll Associates, Mahwah, N.J.

Library of Congress Catalog Card Number: 78-18044
ISBN 0-89375-177-4
ISBN 0-89375-169-3 Paper Edition

921
Coo

Captain James Cook

143071

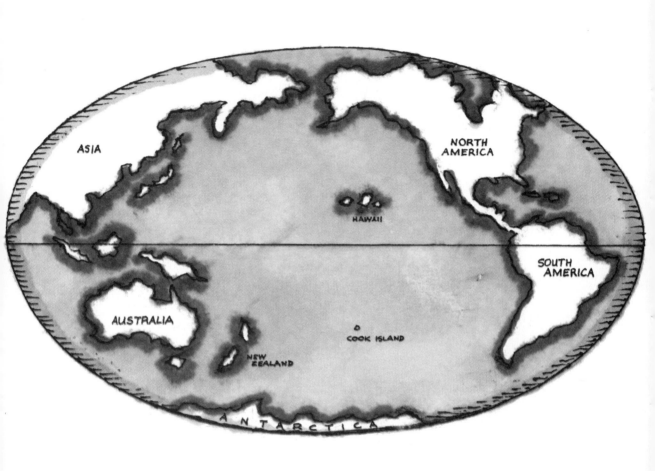

In the year 1745, a Mr. Sanderson, owner of a general store, needed a boy to run errands, sweep the floor, and wait on customers. James Cook, a farm worker, went to see Mr. Sanderson about getting his son the job.

Young James was a tall, handsome boy of 17. He knew nothing about selling groceries and clothing. He had always worked on a farm, taking care of horses and harvesting crops.

Mr. Sanderson quickly discovered that James could read and write. He was also very good with figures. A boy like this would be a big help in his store! The new clerk could sleep under the counter until he found a better place.

There was no way for Mr. Sanderson to know that the boy he had hired to sell ribbons and raisins would become one of the most famous sailors in history. During the next forty years, James Cook would gain fame as a seaman, surveyor, navigator, and mapmaker. He would circle the globe three times. His voyages of discovery would break every record. He would map Pacific islands that Europeans had never seen. He would help find a way to prevent the terrible disease of scurvy. And he would keep journals that, even two hundred years later, are still exciting to read.

Young James, of course, had no idea that such things lay ahead for him. He had spent all his life in farm country. His family had at first expected him to be a farmer. Now his father hoped he would succeed as a merchant.

The town of Staithes, where the young man worked, was a small, busy fishing port on England's seacoast. Mr. Sanderson's store was quite close to the sea.

Every time James looked out the window of the shop, he saw the water. When he wasn't busy, he went to the harbor to watch the boats. He liked the smell of the salt air. He liked the odor of tar the fishermen used to patch their boats. And he listened quietly when sailors talked about ships and sailing. James did not want to be a merchant any more than he wanted to be a farmer! After 18 months at Staithes, he knew he wanted to go to sea.

Fortunately, Mr. Sanderson was an understanding man. He went with James to the nearby seaport of Whitby. Friends of his, John and Robert Walker, built and operated a fleet of coal-carrying ships called *colliers*.

John Walker agreed to take the boy as an apprentice for three years. So James moved in with the Walker family and began to work on the colliers. When he wasn't working or at sea, he was reading and studying mathematics. The Walkers' housekeeper liked James. She brought a table and candles to the attic where he slept so that he could read at night.

At 18, James Cook was over six feet tall, with brown hair and dark eyes. He was much larger and stronger than the other apprentices. Most of them were only 13 or 14.

James quickly became a good sailor. He learned to climb the rigging, hoist the anchor, and steer the ship. He studied charts and learned how to use the compass.

When his three years with the Walker family were finished, James spent two more years sailing in the North Sea on other ships. But when the Walkers asked him to become a mate on one of their new ships, the *Friendship*, he accepted.

After only three years as mate, James was offered command of the *Friendship*. It was a fine opportunity—one any young seaman should be pleased to have. Yet Cook turned it down.

Instead, James Cook, at the age of 27, joined the British Navy. The decision surprised everyone who knew him. The life of a seaman was often far from pleasant. A sailor could expect bad pay, poor food, and the chance of falling ill with scurvy.

But the times were exciting. In 1755, England and France were fighting each other in the Seven Years' War, also called the French and Indian War. Battles took place on both sides of the Atlantic Ocean. Great Britain and France claimed the same territories in North America. Each country built forts in America and got the help of American Indians in defending them.

In Europe, the battles were mostly at sea. The British and French tried to keep each other from sending soldiers, food, and guns to the New World.

In 1757, Cook was ready to take the difficult examinations to become a ship's master. He passed them—and was made master of a new 64-gun ship called the *Pembroke*. The *Pembroke*'s first mission was to take soldiers to Canada.

When Cook reached the mouth of the St. Lawrence River at Quebec, he was given a dangerous assignment. The English needed to capture an important fort that guarded the river. But before an attack could be made, the British had to know more about the river below the fort. Cook and the other masters were told to make charts of the river, including the location of hidden rocks where ships could be wrecked.

Night after night, Cook and the others secretly rowed from their ships to the fort. Again and again, they dropped their weighted lines into the water to measure its depth. Knowing they were well within range of the French guns, they tried to be as quiet as possible. Several times Indians on shore spotted them and shot arrows at them.

In September, 1759, the charts were finished, and the British sailed their large ships up the St. Lawrence. Cook's charts were so accurate that not a ship ran aground. The British attack was successful, and the French fort was taken.

For the next few years, Cook was involved in the war. Finally, he returned to England. In November, 1762, he married a young woman he had known for many years. But even marriage didn't keep him in England long. He was soon given command of a new ship, the *Grenville*.

Cook spent much of the next several years in North American waters. During the summers, he inched his way along the foggy, rocky Canadian shore in small boats. He carefully studied the coasts of Nova Scotia, Cape Breton Island, and Newfoundland, always measuring, inspecting, and taking notes.

During the winters, when his ship was icebound in the harbor at Halifax, Nova Scotia, Cook lived ashore. There he made charts so reliable that they were used to guide ships through Canadian waters for the next one hundred years.

18

James Cook had always been deeply interested in science—especially astronomy. In 1766, he watched an eclipse of the sun. He wrote a paper about it and sent it to the Royal Society of London. The Society was the most respected scientific organization in England. Famous scientists like Isaac Newton belonged to it. The Society thought Cook's paper was excellent and published it.

Two years later, astronomers of the Royal Society announced that in June, 1769, the planet Venus would pass between the earth and the sun.

This was an important happening, and the Society wanted to make sure the event would be observed and recorded. The best place on earth to watch this "Venus transit" was on Tahiti, an island just discovered in the South Pacific. Whom could they send on such a trip?

"What about this man, James Cook?" suggested one member. "Was it not he who sent that fine paper on the sun's eclipse? He would be perfect—for he is both seaman and scientist." Other members agreed, and they sent for Cook.

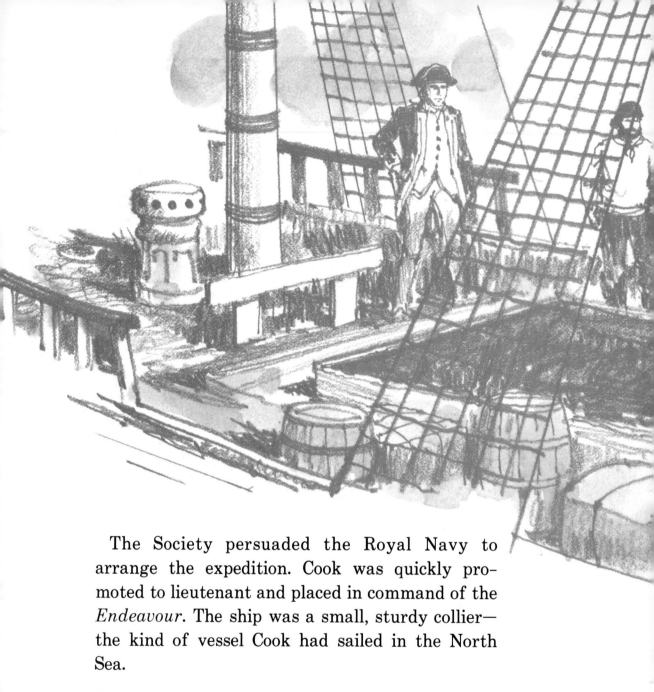

The Society persuaded the Royal Navy to arrange the expedition. Cook was quickly promoted to lieutenant and placed in command of the *Endeavour*. The ship was a small, sturdy collier—the kind of vessel Cook had sailed in the North Sea.

Lieutenant Cook was delighted with his new assignment. He began at once to order supplies that his crew would need for a two-year voyage. Into the *Endeavour*'s roomy hold went a great assortment of food, clothing, medicines, scientific equipment—and trinkets for trading with the Pacific Islanders.

Cook's food supplies were unusual. They included onions and sauerkraut. He knew that after the first few weeks at sea, a sailor's diet consisted mostly of salt beef and dried biscuits. Because ships had no refrigeration, fresh fruits and vegetables could not be kept on board. Many early sailors developed scurvy. They became tired and unable to work. Their gums became swollen. Often their teeth fell out. On long voyages, many men died. Cook believed that the foods he had brought on board would help prevent this disease.

22

Shortly before the *Endeavour* sailed, wealthy young Joseph Banks, whose hobby was natural history, was given permission to come along. With Banks came a party of eight, including two artists, a botanist, a secretary, four servants, two dogs, and a great deal of baggage. Banks planned to study plants, animals, and insects wherever the *Endeavour* went.

This strange shipload of seamen, scientists, servants, and animals sailed from England on August 25, 1768. There was a stop at the Madeira Islands to take on fresh meat, fruit, and vegetables. Each man was given twenty pounds of onions and told to eat them raw—a few each day. Every time there was an opportunity for his men to get fresh food of any kind, Cook made sure that they ate it. He was determined not to lose any men to scurvy.

As they sailed southwest to Rio de Janeiro, Cook recorded his observations of the moon, sun, and stars in his journal. He studied the ocean currents. At Rio, the ship took on supplies and then headed south toward Cape Horn, at the tip of South America.

Near the Horn, he anchored off Tierra del Fuego
so that the men could bring aboard wood and fresh
water. Joseph Banks and his party went ashore
and brought back dozens of plants and flowers for
their artists to sketch. Then the enthusiastic
Banks arranged for an overnight expedition
ashore to collect more specimens. But the weather
changed suddenly, and the party was caught in a
snowstorm. Before they could get back to the ship,
two people froze to death.

After rounding Cape Horn, the *Endeavour* moved northwest. Cook had been told to arrive at Tahiti at least a month before the Venus transit. He was there seven weeks early.

The men of the *Endeavour* were delighted with the friendly people of Tahiti and their beautiful island. Cook and Banks were particularly interested in observing their canoes, houses, and weapons. Both men made many notes in their journals.

Cook set up a small fort on the island and moved his astronomical instruments ashore. But the heavy quadrant, used for measuring the height of stars above the horizon, quickly disappeared. The Tahitians liked objects made of metal. They had spirited it away and taken it apart before anyone knew what had happened. It was some time before all parts of the quadrant were returned.

The weather was excellent. On June 3, 1769, Cook formed three different groups to watch the transit of Venus from various points on the island. Using their instruments, the men recorded the event as carefully as possible.

Afterward, Cook went below to his quarters on the *Endeavour*. From his sea chest, he took out a long sealed envelope. He had been told not to break the seal until his scientific mission had been completed.

Cook broke the seal and read his new orders with great excitement. He was to search for a new land believed to be in the Southern Hemisphere. If he could find it, he was to claim it for England at once and then chart its coastline.

This mysterious "continent" was called *Terra Australis*. Geographers of that time thought that there must be a great body of land in the Southern Hemisphere to "balance" the land masses in the Northern Hemisphere. No one had ever seen it, but explorers from several countries wanted to find it and claim it. Today, we know that such a land does not exist.

Cook sailed from Tahiti on July 13, 1769. Following orders, he went westward, and reached New Zealand.

Some of the tribes of Maoris on New Zealand were friendly. Others were very warlike. After Cook and his sailors discovered that the Maoris were cannibals, they were very careful where they went ashore.

From New Zealand, the *Endeavour* sailed west to New Holland. Cook did not believe that New Holland was the missing *Terra Australis*. But he claimed a large portion of it for England and named it New South Wales. Years later, the country became known as Australia.

Now the *Endeavour* sailed north, staying close to the coast of New Holland for 2,000 miles. Again, Cook made his careful charts. Joseph Banks found many new plants and strange animals, including wallabies, crocodiles, and kangaroos.

Cook was an excellent navigator. But the dangerous Great Barrier Reef near the northeast coast of New Holland almost claimed the ship as a victim. The *Endeavour* became stuck on a jagged piece of coral. To keep it from sinking, the men unloaded much of the cargo. Then they managed to move the ship into a harbor where they made repairs. Exhausted, the crew sailed on. The ship reached the island of Java in the East Indies in October, 1770.

But more trouble awaited them there. Over three years had passed since they had left England. Cook's men had been remarkably healthy up to now. Only eight had died, mostly from accidents. But on Java, some of the sailors caught malaria and other tropical diseases. By the time the ship sailed in December, thirty had died. When the ship reached Cape Town in South Africa three months later, only 56 of the original 94 men were left alive. So Cook had to sign on a new crew for the trip back to England.

Badly in need of repairs, the *Endeavour* made a slow voyage home. She arrived at Dover on July 12, 1771. England hailed the returning Joseph Banks for his scientific discoveries. Some people, however, regarded Cook merely as a "ship driver" who had taken the really important passenger—Banks—around the world!

32

But the Royal Navy rewarded Cook's skill as a captain and a navigator. He was presented to King George III and made a naval commander. He was also told to plan for a second voyage of discovery.

Commander Cook remained ashore for about a year before he set sail on the *Resolution*. She had a companion ship, the *Adventure*, with Lieutenant Tobias Furneaux in command.

The now-famous Joseph Banks planned to sail, too. But he demanded that the *Resolution* be enlarged and made more comfortable for his party of fourteen. This time he even intended to bring along three musicians!

Although Cook believed the *Resolution* was a perfect ship exactly as she was, he was silent while the carpenters made changes. When they had finished, the vessel proved to be top-heavy. She would surely roll over in a strong wind. When the Lords of the Admiralty heard of this, they ordered the new cabins removed. So an angry Joseph Banks and his party were left behind.

34

James Cook's second exploration, one of the greatest single voyages of discovery ever made, began on July 13, 1772. This time he was to approach the South Pole—again in search of Terra Australis.

Although many ships had crossed the Arctic Circle at the North Pole, the weather conditions in the Antarctic, at the South Pole, were far worse. Before 1772, no ship had ever managed to cross the Antarctic Circle. But Commander Cook navigated the *Resolution* and the *Adventure* so well that they succeeded.

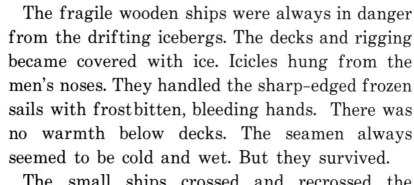

The fragile wooden ships were always in danger from the drifting icebergs. The decks and rigging became covered with ice. Icicles hung from the men's noses. They handled the sharp-edged frozen sails with frostbitten, bleeding hands. There was no warmth below decks. The seamen always seemed to be cold and wet. But they survived.

The small ships crossed and recrossed the Antarctic Circle. Commander Cook wanted to approach the South Pole from as many directions as possible. Whenever he came to a new island, he immediately claimed it for England. Still, he found no land he believed to be Terra Australis.

After each period of exploration, Cook sailed north to warmer climates. He did this so that his men might rest and relax in Tahiti and other islands they had discovered.

In July, 1775, Commander Cook returned to England. On the 60,000-mile voyage, only one man had died of scurvy. The sailors may not have enjoyed eating onions and sauerkraut, but they had returned in good health. Besides his strict rules about food, Cook had insisted on cleanliness, good ventilation, and warm clothing. He prepared a paper for the Royal Society describing the methods he had used to prevent scurvy. For this, he was awarded one of its highest honors and was elected a member of the Society.

James Cook was now promoted to the rank of captain and given a comfortable shore assignment. His wife was pleased. Life had not been easy while her husband had been at sea.

In the spring of 1776, Captain Cook visited his friend, the Earl of Sandwich. The Earl wanted Cook's advice about a voyage of discovery the government was planning. Its purpose was to search for a Northwest Passage from the Pacific, around the continent of North America, to the Atlantic.

London, 1776

With a twinkle in his eye, the Earl asked Cook if he could think of a good captain to lead the expedition. Cook thought a while—then offered to command the voyage himself. The Earl smiled broadly. "Splendid!" he exclaimed. "I had hoped you would go."

Once again, the *Resolution* was made ready for sea. The year was 1776, and England was at war with the American colonies. Shipyards were very busy, and workmen did not always take the time to make repairs properly.

On July 12, 1776, Captain James Cook left England again. The *Discovery* accompanied the *Resolution*. The ships carried many farm animals to be given to the Pacific Islanders.

40

Cook sailed south around the Cape of Good Hope,
then eastward to New Zealand, where he spent the
next year among the islands of the Pacific. Com-
pared with his earlier trips, this voyage
seemed slow and leisurely. Even so, he continued
to make discoveries. On December 24, the ships
came to a bleak little dot of land. Cook promptly
named it Christmas Island.

On January 18, 1778, James Cook made his last major discovery—the group of islands that are now called Hawaii. He named them the Sandwich Islands, after his friend, the Earl.

The people who lived on the islands were friendly. For years, they had believed that one day Lono, the god of peace, happiness, and growing things, would come to them from across the sea. They were sure Cook was that god.

In February, the ships left Hawaii and headed northeast on their search for the passage around North America. The *Resolution* soon needed repairs—probably because of the poor work done in the British shipyards. Two of her masts had to be replaced. The ships anchored at Vancouver Island, near the coast of Canada. The men cut down trees to make the new masts.

Then, continuing north, Cook explored every large river and inlet along the coast of Canada and Alaska. In August, the ships moved into the Bering Strait. Suddenly, the temperature dropped and the weather became stormy. The ships were threatened by ice. If they stayed longer, they might be frozen in until spring. Cook decided to return to Hawaii for the winter.

By now, the word had spread through the islands that Cook *was* the great Lono. As the ships approached the island of Maui, the Hawaiians came out with gifts of fruit and vegetables. Important chiefs came to welcome them. People went aboard and even slept on the ships' decks at night.

On January 16, the two ships entered Kealakekua Bay on the west side of the islands. The following morning, there were over a thousand canoes in the bay. Hundreds of Hawaiians swam around the ships, and thousands more lined the shore.

Cook was pleased that the people were so friendly. He wrote in his journal that the discovery of the islands was one that "seemed in every respect to be the most important made by Europeans throughout . . . the Pacific Ocean."

Those were the last words that he ever wrote in his journal.

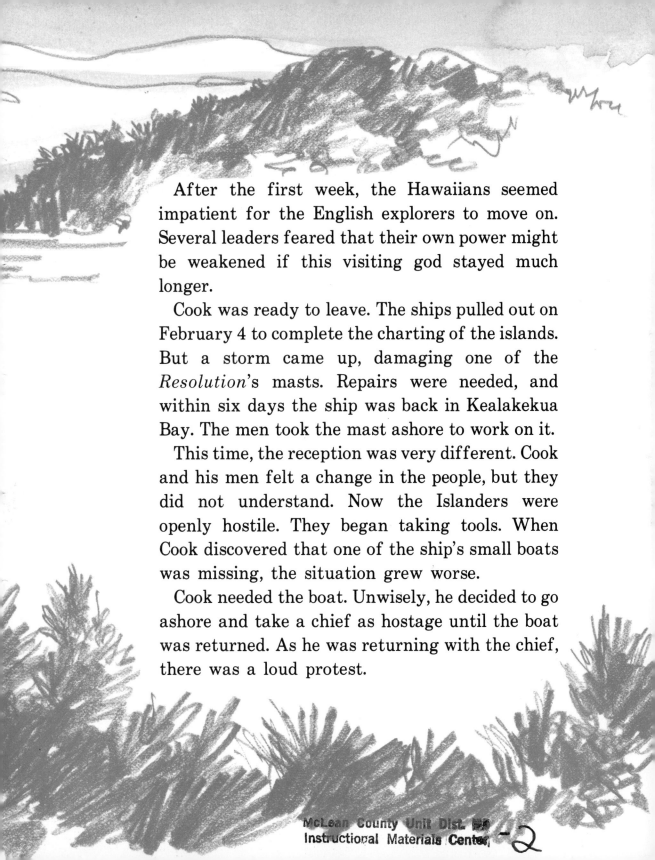

After the first week, the Hawaiians seemed impatient for the English explorers to move on. Several leaders feared that their own power might be weakened if this visiting god stayed much longer.

Cook was ready to leave. The ships pulled out on February 4 to complete the charting of the islands. But a storm came up, damaging one of the *Resolution*'s masts. Repairs were needed, and within six days the ship was back in Kealakekua Bay. The men took the mast ashore to work on it.

This time, the reception was very different. Cook and his men felt a change in the people, but they did not understand. Now the Islanders were openly hostile. They began taking tools. When Cook discovered that one of the ship's small boats was missing, the situation grew worse.

Cook needed the boat. Unwisely, he decided to go ashore and take a chief as hostage until the boat was returned. As he was returning with the chief, there was a loud protest.

McLean County Unit Dist.
Instructional Materials Center

Suddenly, nearly 3,000 Islanders surrounded Cook and his men. A crewman fired, killing one of the chiefs. Then a warrior rushed at Cook with a spear. Cook fired. When he turned to signal his ships, he was hit in the back with a war club. He fell into the water.

Cook died on the beautiful island he had discovered.

Charles Clerke, captain of the *Discovery*, took command. The ships remained at Hawaii while the men repaired the *Resolution*'s mast. The Islanders returned Captain Cook's body, carrying also green palms and white flags of peace.

Captain James Cook was buried in the waters of the bay on February 22, 1779.